Brilliant Activities for

Grammar and Punctuation, Year 3

Activities for Developing and Reinforcing Key Language Skills

Irene Yates

Brilliant
PUBLICATIONS

This set of books is dedicated to the memory of Miss Hannah Gamage and to the children of St. Philip Neri with St. Bede's Catholic Primary School, Mansfield.

● ●

We hope you and your pupils enjoy using the ideas in this book. Brilliant Publications publishes many other books to help primary school teachers. To find out more details on all of our titles, including those listed below, please log onto our website: www.brilliantpublications.co.uk.

Other books in the **Brilliant Activities for Grammar Series**

	Printed version	e-pdf version
Year 1	978-1-78317-125-5	978-1-78317-132-3
Year 2	978-1-78317-126-2	978-1-78317-133-0
Year 4	978-1-78317-128-6	978-1-78317-135-4
Year 5	978-1-78317-129-3	978-1-78317-136-1
Year 6	978-1-78317-130-9	978-1-78317-137-8

Brilliant Activities for Creative Writing Series

Year 1	978-0-85747-463-6
Year 2	978-0-85747-464-3
Year 3	978-0-85747-465-0
Year 4	978-0-85747-466-7
Year 5	978-0-85747-467-4
Year 6	978-0-85747-468-1

Brilliant Activities for Reading Comprehension Series

Year 1	978-1-78317-070-8
Year 2	978-1-78317-071-5
Year 3	978-1-78317-072-2
Year 4	978-1-78317-073-9
Year 5	978-1-78317-074-6
Year 6	978-1-78317-075-3

Published by Brilliant Publications
Unit 10
Sparrow Hall Farm
Edlesborough
Dunstable
Bedfordshire
LU6 2ES, UK

Email: info@brilliantpublications.co.uk
Website: www.brilliantpublications.co.uk
Tel: 01525 222292

The name Brilliant Publications and the logo are registered trademarks.

Written by Irene Yates
Illustrated by Molly Sage
Front cover illustration by Brilliant Publications

Printed ISBN 978-1-78317-127-9
e-pdf ISBN 978-1-78317-134-7

First printed and published in the UK in 2015

The right of Irene Yates to be identified as the author of this work has been asserted by herself in accordance with the Copyright, Designs and Patents Act 1988.

Contents

Introduction 4

Links to the curriculum 5

All about vowels 6

Consonants 7

Articles 8

Which articles? 9

Practising pronouns 10

More pronouns 11

Two problem pronouns 12

Check out some nouns 13

Common noun challenge 14

Proper noun challenge 15

Collections… 16

Lots of collections 17

More collections 18

Preposition puzzle 19

Guess the preposition 20

More prepositions 21

Preposition opposites 22

Conjunctions (1) 23

Conjunctions (2) 24

Simple sentences 25

Subjects and predicates 26

What's a clause? 27

Two clauses 28

Complex sentences 29

It depends 30

Make sentences into a story 31

Adverbs of manner 32

Adverbs of place 33

Adverbs of time 34

Making adverbs 35

Speech bubbles 36

Talking 37

More talking 38

Direct or indirect 39

Which is it? 40

Prefixes 41

Opposites 42

More prefixes 43

Word families are fun! 44

Verb families 45

Find word families 46

Paragraphs 47

Change it 48

Assessment checklist 49

Answers 50–52

Introduction

The **Brilliant Activities for Grammar and Punctuation** series is designed to introduce and reinforce grammatical concepts in line with the National Curriculum Programmes of Study.

The rules of grammar and punctuation are not always easy to access and absorb – or even to teach. It is difficult for children to make the leap from speaking and writing to talking about speaking and writing and to think in the abstract about the words of the language. The ability or readiness to do this requires a certain way of thinking and, for the most part, repetition is the key.

The sheets for this series are all written to add to the children's understanding of these fairly abstract ideas. They aim to improve children's ability to use English effectively and accurately in their own writing and speaking.

The sheets contain oral as well as written contexts because grammar and punctuation are not just about writing. Sometimes the way children have learned to speak is not always grammatically correct but it is the way of speaking that they own. We always have to be aware of instances of regional or familial language and make the point that what we are teaching is what is known universally as 'correct' speech without deprecating the children's own patterns of speech.

The children should always be encouraged to discuss what it is they are learning, to ask questions and to make observations. All of this discussion will help them to understand how the English language works.

The sheets are designed to be structured but flexible so that they can be used to introduce a concept, as stand-alones or as follow-ons. The activities on the sheets can be used as templates to create lots more for practice and reinforcement purposes.

Each book aims to offer:
- groundwork for the introduction of new concepts
- a range of relevant activities
- ideas for continuation
- opportunity for reinforcement
- simple and clear definition of concepts and terms
- opportunities for assessing learning
- clear information for teachers.

Grammar and punctuation can sometimes be a hard grind, but nothing feels so good to a teacher as a pupil, eyes shining, saying, 'Oh, I get that now!' Once they 'get' a concept they never lose it and you can watch it become functional in their writing and, hopefully, hear it become functional in their speaking.

Links to the curriculum

The activity sheets in this series of books will help children to develop their knowledge of Grammar and Punctuation as set out in the Programmes of Study and Appendix 2 of the 2014 National Curriculum for England.

Each book focuses on the concepts to be introduced during that relevant year. Where appropriate, content from previous years is revisited to consolidate knowledge and build on children's understanding.

All about vowels

Look at these words. Underline the ones which have all the vowels.

> The vowels in the alphabet are a, e, i, o and u.

miscellaneous	**education**
mysterious	**mountainous**
cauliflower	**facetious**

Add the missing vowel or vowels and write the word.

__ __ ght (a number) _____

__ r __ ng __ (a fruit _____

f __ r __ w __ y (not close) _____

__ l __ ph __ nt (an animal) _____

__mbr __ ll __ (used in rain) _____

c __ rr __ t (a vegetable) _____

__ l __ __ n (a visitor from space) _____

f __ __ tb __ ll (a game) _____

D __ c __ mb __ r (a month) _____

__ m __ r __ c __ (a place name) _____

Make up some of your own here:

1. _____

2. _____

3. _____

4. _____

> **Go round your group giving an adjective that begins with a vowel for each person's name. Take turns (You can be funny but not rude!)**

The children could play 'I-spy' in small groups but can only use things beginning with a vowel.

Brilliant Activities for Grammar and Punctuation, Year 3
© Irene Yates and Brilliant Publications

Consonants

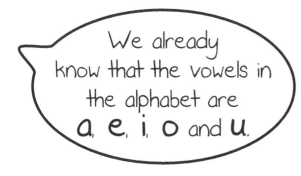

We already know that the vowels in the alphabet are a, e, i, o and u.

The other 21 letters are all consonants. The letter Y is an exception, as it can sometimes be a vowel or a consonant. Like this:

yuk	=	consonant
myth	=	vowel

Every word has to have either a vowel or a 'y' in it somewhere or it would be too difficult to say.

Solve this puzzle by putting in the missing consonants:

1. I'm in the army = __ o __ __ i e __
2. I make bread = __ a __ e __
3. I grow food = __ a __ __ e __
4. I sell meat = __ u __ __ __ e __
5. I fly aeroplanes = __ i __ o __
6. I catch salmon = __ i __ __ e __ __ a __
7. I deliver letters = __ o __ __ __ e __ __ o __
8. I paint pictures = a __ __ i __ __
9. I make you better = __ o __ __ o __
10. I fix cars = __ e __ __ a __ i __

Make up some of your own here:

1. _____
2. _____
3. _____
4. _____

In pairs try to think of as many occupations beginning with a consonant that you can in five minutes.

Get the children skimming and scanning their dictionaries to find words with a 'y' and decide whether it's used as a vowel or a consonant.

Articles

An **article** is the word we put before a noun. There are only three articles in the English language:

a   an   the

The is called the **definite** article because it refers to a specific thing.

The man is next door.   The dog's basket.

A and **an** are called **indefinite** articles because they refer to one of a group of things. **A** is used in front of words beginning with a consonant while **an** is used in front of words beginning with a vowel. Fill in the blanks.

___ man is next door.   It's ___ dog's basket.

___ bird   ___ apple   ___ baby

___ boy   ___ ostrich   ___ elephant

Try to tell your partner about where you live without using the definite article 'the'. Can you do it?

If pupils speak or are learning other languages, you could talk about how other languages have more (or less) articles.

Brilliant Activities for Grammar and Punctuation, Year 3
© Irene Yates and Brilliant Publications

Which articles?

Can you complete this story using **definite** and **indefinite** articles?

I was on _____ picnic trip to _____ park. In my lunch box there was ____ apple, ____ banana, ____ sandwich and ____ little pack of cheese. _____ cheese was so hard to open, I knocked _____ whole lunch box to _____ ground and everything spilled out. ____ goose came up from nowhere. It snatched up ____ sandwich in its beak and waddled off. ____ duck came to see what it could find. It found ____ bit of ham, but as it dangled from its beak ____ different goose grabbed it from _____ duck and made off with it.

Find five nouns that start with a vowel and five adjectives that start with a vowel then find five nouns and five adjectives that start with a consonant.

Spend time reading the paragraph together before the children fill in the articles.

Practising pronouns

Read this sentence aloud.

Jane said Jane couldn't go to the party because Jane's mother couldn't take Jane.

What's wrong with it?

Some of the nouns need to change to pronouns, like this:

Jane said <u>she</u> couldn't go to the party because <u>her</u> mother couldn't take <u>her</u>.

Here are some pronouns:

I	**we**	**me**	**us**	**you**	**he**
it	**they**	**him**	**her**	**them**	**she**

Write some sentences using at least two of these pronouns in each **one**.

_____

_____

_____

_____

_____

> **Think up silly sentences that have no pronouns – how complicated a sentence can you make?**

Do plenty of verbal work, shooting a pronoun (or two) at the children for them to make up on the spot silly sentences.

More pronouns

Remembering that pronouns take the place of nouns, read these sentences, decide which pronoun is correct and add it in.

1. Stephen's mum gave _____ a packet of biscuits.
(her, him, it)

2. Jay wasn't at school because _____ was ill. (her, me, she)

3. Did _____ get the homework? (us, you, me)

4. Will you come with _____ ? (she, he, me)

5. Are _____ going to help? (he, I, they)

6. Hannah said _____ was very tired. (it, she, you)

7. Sally asked the boy to get _____ an ice-cream.
(him, her, it)

8. The book is Ian's – give it back to _____. (she, I, him)

> **Is it possible to make up sentences aloud with the wrong pronouns in them? Try it. One talks, one spots, then swap.**

Before doing the task, read some passages aloud from a story and have the children call out when they hear a pronoun.

Two problem pronouns

Sometimes it's hard to decide if it should be **I** or **me** in a sentence. Here is a trick that will help you to know and get it right every time.

Take the sentence below for example. If you split the sentence into two short sentences, like this, which parts sound better?

Ryan and (I/me) are going to the circus.

Ryan is going to the circus.

{ I am going to the circus. ✔

Me am going to the circus. ✘

So the correct version is Ryan and I ...

What about this one?

Dad told Jack and (I/me) to turn the TV off.

Dad told Jack ...

{ Dad told I to turn the TV off. ✘

Dad told me to turn the TV off. ✔

So the correct version is Dad told Jack and me to ...

Try these:

1. Mum and _____ (I, me) went shopping.

2. _____ (I, me) and my sister went to the park.

3. The dog and _____ (I, me) ate the biscuits together.

4. Mum told my brother and _____ (I, me) to pick up our litter.

Make up some more sentences using *I* and *me*.

> **Listen to each other talking; spot the errors! Lots of people use 'me' when they should use 'I'. Now you can tell them why they're wrong. You wouldn't say 'me am going to the circus', would you?**

Get the children to verbalise lots of examples using 'I' and 'me'.

Brilliant Activities for Grammar and Punctuation, Year 3
© Irene Yates and Brilliant Publications

Check out some nouns

Make sure you know what a noun is. Think about common nouns and proper nouns.

What is the difference?

Name four things you might find in:

a car	a toy shop	a kitchen

a cinema	a church	a hospital

Name four things that are proper nouns for each of these:

Countries	People	Days of the week

In five minutes name as many things you can find in a safari park as you can.

Do lots of verbal revision to make sure children understand the terms 'common noun' and 'proper noun' and the difference when writing them.

Common noun challenge

You know what common nouns are.

Get your dictionaries out and, in 20 minutes, write:

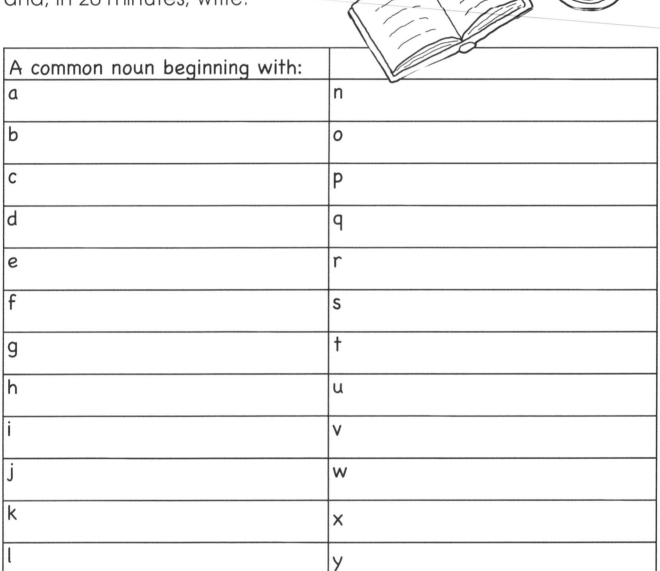

A common noun beginning with:	
a	n
b	o
c	p
d	q
e	r
f	s
g	t
h	u
i	v
j	w
k	x
l	y
m	z

Compare your results with your partner's. How many do you share?

Make sure the children have simple dictionaries that they can use. They could fill in all the ones they can do without using a dictionary first, then look for the rest. Change the time period to be appropriate for your pupils. Challenge them to find unusual common nouns that no one else has thought of.

Brilliant Activities for Grammar and Punctuation, Year 3
© Irene Yates and Brilliant Publications

Proper noun challenge

You know what proper nouns are.

Get your dictionaries out
and, in 20 minutes, write:

A proper noun beginning with:	
A	N
B	O
C	P
D	Q
E	R
F	S
G	T
H	U
I	V
J	W
K	X
L	Y
M	Z

Compare your results with your partner's. How many do you share?

Make sure the children have simple dictionaries that they can use. They could fill in all the ones they can do without using a dictionary first, then look for the rest. Change the time period to be appropriate for your pupils. Challenge them to find unusual proper nouns that no one else has thought of.

Collections

Here's another type of noun. It is called a <u>collective</u> noun.

A **collective** noun is a word which describes a group. The collective noun for a group of <u>dogs</u> is a **pack**

a pack of dogs,   a flock of birds, a class of children

Which nouns describe these collections?

apples, pears, bananas = _____

tables, chairs, cupboards = _____

ants, bees, crickets = _____

robins, sparrows, magpies = _____

Make up some imaginary collective nouns for:

snakes =   a _____ of snakes

frogs =   a _____ of frogs

elephants =   a _____ of elephants

dolphins =   a _____ of dolphins

giraffes =   a _____ of giraffes

hyenas =   a _____ of hyenas

> **Have fun making up imaginary collective nouns for: teachers, games, shoes, burgers, siblings.**

Draw a large template shape, eg a bird/an insect. The children cut out the large shape and fill it with words or pictures of those things that belong in the group. Use for display.

Brilliant Activities for Grammar and Punctuation, Year 3
© Irene Yates and Brilliant Publications

Lots of collections

Write each noun under its collective heading:

nine	cow	pants	sparrow	bee
coffee	grandad	cabbage	two	rugby
parsnip	aunt	lemonade	daffodil	wren
wasp	basketball	jacket	dog	one
horse	shirt	hawk	ant	tulip
petrol	cousin	donkey	forty	rose
niece	turnip	football	carrot	golf
wine	daisy	fly	thrush	dress

Birds	Liquids	Family	Games
Numbers	**Clothes**	**Vegetables**	**Flowers**
Insects	**Animals**		

How many things can you think of in five minutes that come under the group 'food'?

Make sure children can read all the words. When the task is done, ask for two more groups for the empty boxes and challenge them to find at least four things for each.

More collections

Write in each box the word that names each group, collection or class of items:

man woman girl dad sister baby _____	elm oak willow ash alder beech _____
USA Spain France Russia Brazil Italy _____	chips chop sausage turkey spaghetti apple _____
lettuce tomato radish onion cucumber cress _____	ring necklace bracelet pearls earrings pendant _____

Can you complete these?

a class of _____   a swarm of _____

a team of _____   a string of _____

a bunch of _____   a pack of _____

> ## Take it in turns to think of nouns that come under the groups of furniture and insects.

Talk through first. Make sure the children have dictionaries to help with their spelling of these group names.

Brilliant Activities for Grammar and Punctuation, Year 3
© Irene Yates and Brilliant Publications

Preposition puzzle

Prepositions tell us the position of things, like this:

The dog is <u>in</u> his box. Or **The boy is <u>under</u> his bed.**

Sometimes prepositions are called 'place' words. Make up a funny sentence for each of these prepositions:

on

_____

with

_____

into

_____

over

_____

under

_____

down

_____

in

_____

> **Play 'spot the prep'. One talks, the other counts and writes down the prepositions used, then swap. How many have you used in one discussion?**

Have the children use their dictionaries to list as many prepositions (prep) as they can. There are about 150 prepositions in the English language and we use them constantly. How many can they recognise in their own writing?

Guess the preposition

In your workbook write sentences that describe what's happening in these pictures. Remember to use prepositions.

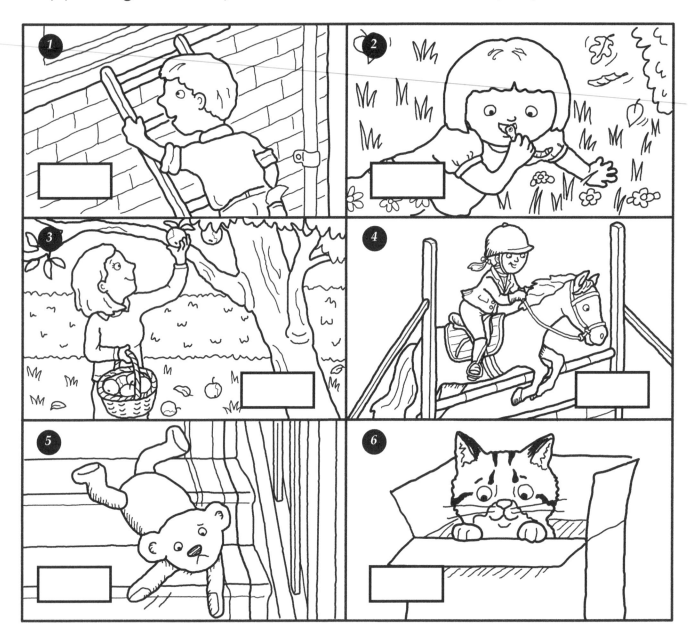

Draw three pictures that illustrate 'around', 'through' and 'between', and write a sentence for each.

> **Give a set of instructions for your friend to carry out, for example, 'Put your bag under the table.' Swap.**

*Have a large display picture. Ask the children questions – where is the table? The table is **in** the room.*

Brilliant Activities for Grammar and Punctuation, Year 3
© Irene Yates and Brilliant Publications

More prepositions

Prepositions show the relationship of a noun or pronoun to another word in the sentence, like this:

The girls had a picnic <u>near</u> the stables.

Use one of the prepositions shown to complete these sentences:

through   **on**   **over**   **in**   **up**   **under**

The girls walked _____ the fields. A fox jumped

_____ the fence. There was a hedgehog

_____ a bush. There was a bird's nest

_____ a tree. They climbed _____ a

steep hill and laid the picnic blanket _____ the

ground.

Continue the story, using as many of these prepositions as you can:

for   **at**   **with**   **from**   **after**

_____

_____

_____

_____

Read your story to a partner.

> **Verbalise the sentences you want to write for the story and check they include prepositions before you begin to write them down.**

Discuss the prepositions in this task and then ask the children to try to find opposites for them. For example: on / off.

Preposition opposites

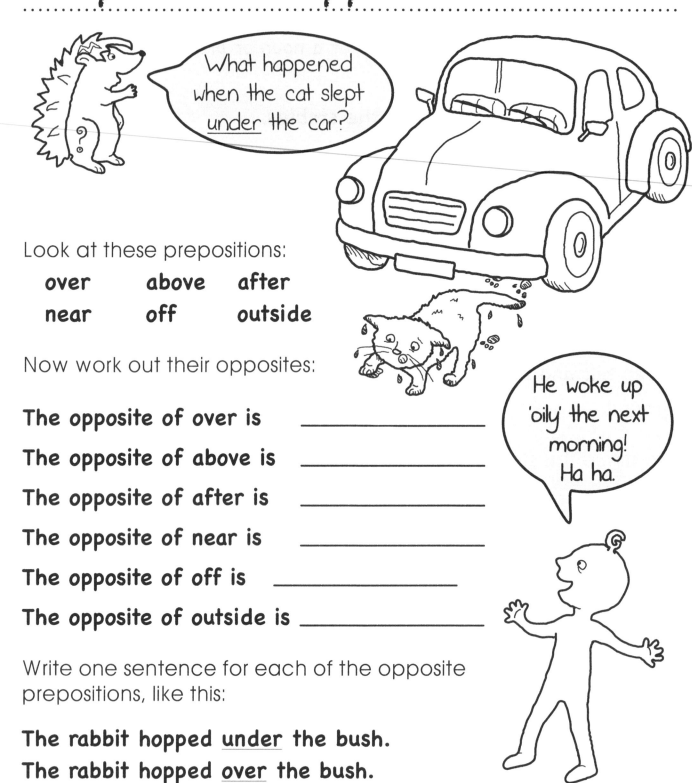

Speech bubble: What happened when the cat slept <u>under</u> the car?

Speech bubble: He woke up 'oily' the next morning! Ha ha.

Look at these prepositions:

over	**above**	**after**
near	**off**	**outside**

Now work out their opposites:

The opposite of over is _____

The opposite of above is _____

The opposite of after is _____

The opposite of near is _____

The opposite of off is _____

The opposite of outside is _____

Write one sentence for each of the opposite prepositions, like this:

The rabbit hopped <u>under</u> the bush.

The rabbit hopped <u>over</u> the bush.

Challenge: in pairs, one gives a preposition, the other gives its opposite. Take turns.

Get the children to make up verbal sentences containing: behind/ in front of, into/ out of, outside/ inside, etc before they do the writing task.

Conjunctions (1)

Conjunctions are joining words. We use them to show time, place or cause, like this:

We laughed **when** the dog fell off the chair.

We clean our teeth **before** we go to bed.

I can't come out **because** I'm not very well.

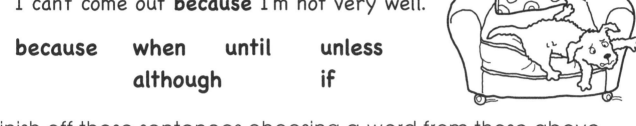

because   **when**   **until**   **unless**

although   **if**

Finish off these sentences choosing a word from those above.

We had to wait _____ the baby cried.

The kitten won't come to you _____ you call it.

Dad said it would be all right _____ she bought the apple.

I will be there _____ I'll be late.

Join together the sentences below with one of these conjunctions. Write your sentences in your workbook or on a separate sheet.

but   **because**   **if**   **since**   **so**

I cannot lift the bag. It is too heavy.

We'll have to dig our way out. It just keeps snowing.

He hasn't phoned me. I told him to go home.

We felt cold. We put the heating on.

The train was late. We got there on time.

Jaz can't come. She is grounded.

> **All these sentences have been joined in the middle.**
> **What happens if you use a conjunction at the beginning?**
> **Experiment with doing this.**

*Explain that many words that are conjunctions are also prepositions. What counts is what they do within the sentence. These words are all **joining** parts of sentences, so they are conjunctions.*

Conjunctions (2)

Conjunctions are words used to join two short sentences together, to make a larger one.
For example,

because   **Tom had a shower <u>because</u> he was muddy.**

Write sentences using these conjunctions.

when
_____

so
_____

and
_____

before
_____

if
_____

because
_____

unless
_____

Can you make your sentences into a story?

Go through a piece of text together looking for all the joining words.

Talk and verbalise lots of examples of conjunctions before the children complete the activity.

Brilliant Activities for Grammar and Punctuation, Year 3
© Irene Yates and Brilliant Publications

Simple sentences

Sentences can be simple, compound or complex.

A simple sentence has a **subject** (a noun - what the sentence is about) and a **verb**. A simple sentence will make sense on its own.

The simplest sentences have just two words. For example:

Cats purr.

subject ↗ ↖ verb

(someone or something)   (what the subject is doing, will do or did)

Can you split these simple sentences into subjects and verbs. Just think, what does what?

	Subject	Verb
Babies cry.		
Boys climb.		
Girls giggle.		
Teachers teach.		
Children learn.		
Trees grow.		
Fish swim.		
Ducks quack.		
Rain pours.		
The Sun shines.		

Think of a verb. How many different subjects might be able to do it? Think of a subject – how many verbs can you think of to follow it?

Ask for lots of verbal examples. Simple sentences can, of course, be much longer; the only requirement is that they have just one clause (ie, verb). You could ask children to extend the sentences by adding an adjective (eg Hungry babies cry), a noun (eg Boys climb trees) or a noun phrase (Trees grow in our garden).

Subjects and predicates

Sentences have two parts: the subject tells us who or what something is and the predicate has a verb and tells us what they did.

The frog (**subject**) hopped into the pond (**predicate**)

These sentences are muddled up. Draw lines to match the correct subjects and their predicates. Underline the verbs.

Dinosaurs	**came to school on his bike.**
You	**are yellow.**
A snake	**must not be late for school.**
The teacher	**is long and slithery.**
Bananas	**gave us gold stars for our work.**
My friend	**are extinct.**

Add a predicate for each subject. Underline the verbs.

Aliens _

The police officer _ _ _ _ _ _ _ _ _ _ _ _ _ _ _ _

The motor bike _ _ _ _ _ _ _ _ _ _ _ _ _ _ _ _ _

Tom's mum _ _ _ _ _ _ _ _ _ _ _ _ _ _ _ _ _ _

Sophie _ _ _ _ _ _ _ _ _ _ _ _ _ _ _ _ _ _ _

I _

Tell each other three sentences of something you did, saw or watched yesterday. Split the sentences into two parts.

Talk about the sentences. Make sure the children understand which word is the verb in each and that the predicate contains the verb. They need not get hung up on the terms 'subject' and 'predicate'.

Brilliant Activities for Grammar and Punctuation, Year 3
© Irene Yates and Brilliant Publications

What's a clause?

There's a word we need to understand that is related to sentences.

It's the word <u>clause</u>. Not claws, which are animals' toes and not Claus as in Santa. A <u>clause</u> is a group of words that contains a <u>verb</u> and makes sense on its own.
Like this:

I <u>ate</u> (verb) the cake.

I <u>dropped</u> (verb) the milk.

The dog <u>chased</u> (verb) the cat.

A simple sentence is made up of **one clause**. Remember – the sentence must have a verb and it must make sense all by itself. If it has **more than one verb**, it is **not** a simple sentence.

Finish these simple sentences:

I like _ _ _ _ _ _ _ _ _ _ _

We went _ _ _ _ _ _ _ _ _

The giraffe _ _ _ _ _ _ _ _

They wanted _ _ _ _ _ _ _ _

Who said _ _ _ _ _ _ _ _ _

Are you _ _ _ _ _ _ _ _ _

When will _ _ _ _ _ _ _ _

She would like _ _ _ _ _ _ _

> **Discuss the idea of 'clause'. Can you explain to each other and give examples?**

Simple sentences can be questions as well as statements. The trick is for the children to recognise the verb, eg Are you going to school? The verb is <u>are going</u>. Lots of talk is needed!

Two clauses

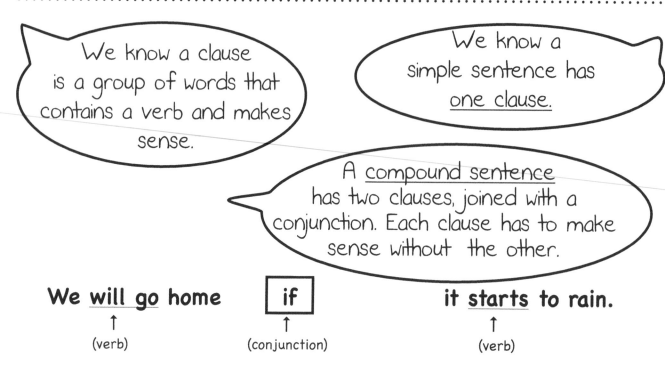

We will go home if it starts to rain.

The two clauses are joined by a conjunction. Remember – each clause has to make sense without the other one.

Circle the conjunctions in these sentences. Underline the verbs:

I had ten books and I read them in the holidays.

I like oranges but I love bananas.

Their coats got wet when it poured with rain.

Our class went on a trip and we had a great time.

Make up four compound sentences of your own and write them in your workbook or on a piece of paper. (Check each clause makes sense on its own. Check they are joined with a conjunction.)

With a partner choose some conjunctions. One makes up one clause plus the conjunction, then the other finishes the sentence with another clause. Take turns.

Understanding these concepts takes lots of discussion and experimentation. Try to make a challenge out of it.

Brilliant Activities for Grammar and Punctuation, Year 3
© Irene Yates and Brilliant Publications

Complex sentences

When sentences have more than one clause, and only one of the clauses makes sense on its own, it is called a complex sentence.

The clause that makes sense on its own is called the **main clause**. The clause that doesn't make sense on its own is called a **dependent** or **subordinate clause**, because it depends on the main clause to make sense. Like this:

The burgers are tasty and so are the fries.

       ↑   ↑

Main clause   dependent or subordinate clause

'The burgers are tasty' is the main clause, because 'and so are the fries' doesn't make sense without it.

The picnic was great until it rained.

The police chased the robbers who broke into the shop.

When it stops raining, we'll be able to play out.

Pick out and underline the main clauses in these sentences:

Jimmy ruined his shoes when he paddled in them.

We went to the circus and saw the elephants dancing.

The boy, who broke his leg, hobbled down the street. (Be careful!)

We all got wet when it rained.

When it snowed, we built snowmen. (Be careful!)

> **What kind of sentences do you use most when you chat? Complex? Simple? Compound? Try to work it out.**

Subordinate clauses do not necessarily come at the ends of sentences, they can come at the beginning or in the middle of a sentence. Read a common text together and play 'spot the clause' – is it a main clause or a subordinate?

It depends ...

A subordinate clause adds information to a main clause.

Why did the music teacher need a ladder?

To reach the high notes! Ha ha.

Here are some subordinate clauses. You need to add a main clause to each one to make a proper complex sentence.

after the bell went _____

_____

because she was tired _____

_____

that come from outer space _____

_____

who gave the prize _____

_____

which was the best _____

_____

that grew in the garden _____

_____

> ### Look through comics to find main clauses and subordinate clauses.

Look for subordinate clauses in texts that the children are familiar with; point them out and discuss how they add meaning to the sentence that contains them.

Brilliant Activities for Grammar and Punctuation, Year 3
© Irene Yates and Brilliant Publications

Make sentences into a story

I am giving you:

a dog	a bus driver	a basket of shopping

a smile	a scream	and a sunny day

You can have anything, or anyone else to add to your story.

Write the story, making sure you have at least:

1 simple sentence   1 compound sentence   1 complex sentence

_____

_____

_____

_____

_____

_____

_____

_____

_____

_____

Work out what the rest of the sentences are after you've finished.

Discuss what you think might happen in the story. Help each other with ideas for plotting it.

Have lots of talk about this activity; recap on clauses and different kinds of sentences. Help the children to verbalise before writing.

Adverbs of manner

Adverbs are really useful words. They tell us more about an adjective, a verb or another adverb.

Like this: **The boy ran quickly.**
Quickly tells us **how** the boy ran so it is an adverb of manner.

Here are some adverbs of manner; they all tell us how something is happening:

noisily   **easily**   **slowly**   **silently**

gently   **carefully**   **proudly**   **sadly**

These adverbs tell more about verbs, for example, we might say write neatly, or play noisily, etc.

Write a sentence for each adverb.

_____

_____

_____

_____

_____

_____

_____

> **Talk about things you can do, for example, jump, hop, skip. Think of adverbs that might describe how you would do these things.**

Have lots of talk about verbs that might be appropriate with each adverb, before the children complete the activity. Give them opportunity to verbalise their ideas.

Brilliant Activities for Grammar and Punctuation, Year 3
© Irene Yates and Brilliant Publications

Adverbs of place

An adverb tells us more about an adjective, a verb or another adverb, like this:

I told you to come <u>here</u>!

<u>Here</u> tells us **where** the person who's speaking wants whoever he is speaking to, to be.

<u>Here</u> tells us the place. It is an adverb of <u>place</u>.

Here are some adverbs of place that tell us where.

| out | here | there | somewhere |
| in | near | far away | everywhere |

Write a sentence for each adverb.

_____

_____

_____

_____

_____

_____

_____

**Think up sentences together for:
above, below, downstairs, behind, in front of.**

Discuss all the place adverbs that the children can think of. Give them plenty of time to verbalise their sentences before they write them down.

Adverbs of time

Adverbs tell us more about an adjective, a verb or another adverb. Like this:

He played with me <u>yesterday</u>.

<u>Yesterday</u> tells us **when** they played. It is an adverb of <u>time</u>.

Here are some adverbs of time that tell us when something happened or is going to happen.

later	now	often	before
then	**today**	**soon**	**never**

Write a sentence for each adverb.

_____

_____

_____

_____

_____

_____

_____

> **Think up sentences together for already, seldom, tomorrow, next year, soon.**

Have lots of discussion about all the time adverbs the children can think of. Give them plenty of time to verbalise their sentences before they write them down.

Brilliant Activities for Grammar and Punctuation, Year 3
© Irene Yates and Brilliant Publications

Making adverbs

You can change adjectives into adverbs very easily, like this:

**If the cat is <u>greedy</u> (adjective) – you can say
the cat eats <u>greedily</u> (adverb)**

**If the boy is <u>noisy</u> – you can say
the boy plays <u>noisily</u>.**

Write some pairs of sentences using these adjectives and adverbs:

sad, sadly _____

_____

angry, angrily _____

_____

quick, quickly _____

_____

slow, slowly _____

_____

curious, curiously _____

_____

> **Have a look at a piece of text together and see if you can pick out all the adverbs of how, when and where.**

Talk about other adjectives that can be changed into adverbs that add meaning to a verb. The trick to recognising them is: an adjective always refers to a noun. An adverb refers to an adjective, a verb or another adverb.

Speech bubbles

When you write a comic strip, all of the people speak in speech bubbles. Like this:

Hi Lucy. How are you today?

OK, but I've got sooo much homework to do!

A spaceship lands in the playground at playtime. Write the story of the alien's visit using pictures and speech bubbles.

Have a conversation with a friend. Draw imaginary speech bubbles in the air round what you both say.

Find as many comics, magazines etc, with speech bubbles as you can to share with the children so that they all understand exactly how a speech bubble works.

Brilliant Activities for Grammar and Punctuation, Year 3
© Irene Yates and Brilliant Publications

Talking

When we write down someone talking we can do it with a speech bubble, like this:

Or with punctuation marks, like this:

"Where are you going?" Joe said.

The punctuation marks " " (or ' ') are sometimes called **speech marks** or **quotation marks**. Whatever you call them, they're just the same as a speech bubble. You never write the 'he said' bit inside the speech marks because you wouldn't do that in a speech bubble, would you?

Put these speech bubbles into sentences with quotation marks:

Can you make your sentences into a story?

Get into groups. Find a story with some speech in it and act out the parts.

Take an exchange of dialogue from a comic or magazine. Blow it up and re-write it as text with the children, to demonstrate.

More talking

Here's a little story with lots of talking in it.

Make it into a cartoon with speech bubbles. You may want to put captions under your pictures.

"Okay," said Mum. "Everybody ready? We're going shopping."

Jack groaned, "Oh no!"

Mum said, "Stop making a fuss, Jack. Bring the shopping bags."

"Come on Jack," piped up his sister, Millie. "I don't see why I should have to go if you don't."

"He is coming," Mum said. "He's the only one tall enough to reach the top shelves."

"And," Millie said, "he's the one who eats all the food."

"Gerroff!" said Jack.

Tell the next bit of the story in your own words, using speech where you can.

If the children can equate direct speech with speech bubbles, they can understand the concept of quotation/speech marks when it's pointed out to them.

Brilliant Activities for Grammar and Punctuation, Year 3
© Irene Yates and Brilliant Publications

Direct or indirect

So now we know all about quotation/speech marks there just has to be a complication. The words in speech marks are called **direct speech**. There is another kind of speech that doesn't need speech marks at all. This is called **indirect speech**.

This is how indirect speech works:

Jack said he didn't want to go shopping.
To change this into direct speech you would have to write:
Jack said, "I don't want to go shopping."

Which of these is which? Tick the correct box.

	Direct	Indirect
"But I don't want to," Jack grumbled.		
Mum said that was tough but he still had to go.		
Millie said he needed to get a grip.		
"I'll be too tired to play football with my mates," Jack moaned.		
"Anyway, shopping's boring."		
"It's boring for me as well," Mum snapped.		
"And if there's nothing to eat you'll be moaning even more," Millie said.		
Jack said he'd go but they'd have to wait while he got ready and texted his friend that he'd be late.		
"Just get a move on, will you?" Mum said.		

One person makes a statement or asks a question; the other says it as indirect speech. Take turns.

Get the children to work out lots of examples of direct and indirect speech and verbalise them to the class.

Which is it?

Each of these examples is direct speech or indirect speech. Decide which it is and then change it to the opposite.

1. "It's too hot today," said Sahid.

    _____

2. "I hate chocolate," Maura said.

    _____

3. Mum asked who my friend was.

    _____

4. Ayesha said she'd been grounded.

    _____

5. "What is it for?" asked Sophie.

    _____

6. Sam's dad told Tom that Sam was not well.

    _____

7. "My favourite food is broccoli," Millie said.

    _____

8. "Yuck!" exclaimed James.

    _____

9. The boy couldn't understand why she was surprised.

    _____

10. Sam's dad said, "I'll take you to the match anyway."

    _____

> ## Together, look for examples of indirect speech in texts. It's easier to spot the speech marks!

Recap the meaning of direct and indirect speech. Recap how it is written. Make sure all children can read the sentences but encourage them to complete the activity autonomously.

Prefixes

Lots of words begin with the same set of letters. Like this:

trio   **triangle**   **triple**   **tripod**   **tricycle**   **triplet**

Find out what these words mean using your dictionary. What do you notice?

You should see that all the words begin with **tri** and **tri** means three.

When we add letters like tri to the beginning of words it is called a prefix (pre means 'before') and a prefix can help to make new words and change others.

Find out what these prefixes mean and then find as many words as you can that begin with them. (Tip: each one has something to do with numbers.)

cent
oct
mille
duo

Use a dictionary together to try to find words for the task.

The children should be able to work out verbally the meaning of these four prefixes by inputting examples and discussing them. You can then call for example words before they do the written task.

Opposites

Some prefixes can make words which mean the opposite of the original words. Like this:

un + **happy** = **unhappy**
(prefix) (word)

dis + **appear** = _____

anti + **climax** = _____

in + **capable** = _____

Find one more word to go with each of these prefixes:

un _____ **dis** _____

anti _____ **in** _____

You can add one of these prefixes to all of these words. Which is it? Write out the new words:

seen _____ **tie** _____

real _____ **willing** _____

do _____ **paid** _____

roll _____ **steady** _____

wise _____ **safe** _____

Which prefix can you add to these?

agree _____ **like** _____

trust _____ **honest** _____

Can you think of any words that begin with the prefix 'non'?

Challenge the children to write all the words they can think of that begin with one or more of the prefixes. Give them a time limit of 15 minutes.

Brilliant Activities for Grammar and Punctuation, Year 3
© Irene Yates and Brilliant Publications

More prefixes

The trick with a prefix is to find out what it means and then see how many words you can add to it in order to make nouns. Look at these prefixes. First of all, decide what you **think** they mean and then find out if you are right or wrong.

super – for example, supermarket

auto – for example, automobile

anti – for example, antibiotic

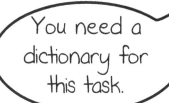

You need a dictionary for this task.

	super	auto	anti
This is what I think it means:			
This is what it does mean:			
Words I have found:			

Think of words that are nouns beginning with the prefix 'tele'. Find out what 'tele' means.

Make this activity a 'using the dictionary' task. Talk through the instructions. Revisit dictionary rules.

Word families are fun!

Word families show how words can be related to each other and help us with spellings and meanings.

There are two kinds of word family.

The first is: they are similar in how they are formed.

word   **worded**   **wordy**

The second is: their meanings have something in common.

big   **little**   **size**
cat   **whisker**   **tail**

With word families you have to look and see what you think they have in common. See how many words you can add to these families:

run, ran, _____

nest, hive _____

said, called _____

bicycle, skateboard _____

jump, jumping _____

jump, hop _____

write, written _____

rose, daffodil _____

In five minutes see how many words you can find for a word family of 'pet'.

Use some of the examples to make a display chart, cutting pictures from magazines to stick and turn into a collage for meaning, using text for form.

Brilliant Activities for Grammar and Punctuation, Year 3
© Irene Yates and Brilliant Publications

Verb families

All of these words are verbs and each belongs to a family. Join all the verbs that are related to each other.

run	swam	trots	bounced
climb	skates	climbing	jog
running	trotting	swimming	jogging
skating	bounces	ran	trotted
swims	trot	bouncing	skated
runs	swim	jogs	skate
climbs	jogged	bounce	climbed

How many families can you find?

_____   _____

_____   _____

_____   _____

_____   _____

_____   _____

Find one other physical activity each and work out as many words as you can to fit in the verb family.

Talk about word families. These words are familiar of form.

Brilliant Activities for Grammar and Punctuation, Year 3
© Irene Yates and Brilliant Publications

This page may be photocopied for use by the purchasing institution only.

45

Find word families

Collect some comics, printed booklets or pages from the supermarket or other places. Look for interesting word families. Give each group or family a heading and cut and stick them into the right place.

Families you might look for are:

Words that sound like noises	Words that name wild animals	Words with the **oo** sound
Words …	Words …	Words …

How many words can you say that belong to the punctuation family?

Give the children several ideas – eg twin or pairs of words (salt and pepper); words that have more than one meaning (last, felt); words for an environment (seaside, countryside). Get the children to offer lots more.

Brilliant Activities for Grammar and Punctuation, Year 3
© Irene Yates and Brilliant Publications

Paragraphs

The reason we write in paragraphs is to keep the text clear and easy to read. If you are reading a huge chunk of text on a page and there is no white space between the lines it gets very hard to read:

If you are reading a huge chunk of text on a page and there is no white space between the lines it gets very hard to read. If you are reading a huge chunk of text on a page and there is no white space between the lines it gets very hard to read. If you are reading a huge chunk of text on a page and there is no white space between the lines it gets very hard to read. If you are reading a huge chunk of text on a page and there is no white space between the lines it gets very hard to read. If you are reading a huge chunk of text on a page and there is no white space between the lines it gets very hard to read. If you are reading a huge chunk of text on a page and there is no white space between the lines it gets very hard to read.

If you are reading a huge chunk of text on a page and there is no white space between the lines it gets very hard to read. If you are reading a huge chunk of text on a page and there is no white space between the lines it gets very hard to read.

If you are reading a huge chunk of text on a page and there is no white space between the lines it gets very hard to read. If you are reading a huge chunk of text on a page and there is no white space between the lines it gets very hard to read.

If you are reading a huge chunk of text on a page and there is no white space between the lines it gets very hard to read.

As you can see text with paragraphs is easier because it has white space in between. You start a new paragraph when you start a new topic, for instance, if the time changes, the subject changes, or a different character is introduced.

To start a new paragraph you start a new line. When writing by hand you should also leave a word space at the beginning of the first line of the paragraph.

Search a magazine or newspaper to find large chunks of text without paragraphs and large chunks with. Cut and stick them in your workbook or on a separate sheet of paper.

> **Pick up some library books at random and go through them together looking for paragraphs. Do the flick test on choosing books to read. Which ones 'catch your eye' best?**

Give the children an example of a story they know, or part of a reference text they know, but take the paragraphing out and ask them to put the breaks in.

Change it

Most of the time when we write stories we write them in the past tense, like this:

Izzy decided to make some cakes for her mum, but what a mess she made! Mum was absolutely furious. The kitchen looked like someone has had a food fight in it.

But we can write stories in another way, pretending we are in the present moment. Sometimes we talk like that. We are telling someone what happened yesterday, but we say, 'And he's like, going mad at me and I'm trying to apologise but....'

So we would write:

Izzy has decided she'll make some cakes for her mum but now she has made a mess. Her mum is furious because the kitchen is now looking as if someone is having a food fight in it.

Copy a piece of text that's in the past tense, then rewrite it, in the same way: the tense is called <u>present perfect</u>.

> **Tell an anecdote of something that happened to you but tell it as if it is happening now. Take turns with your friend.**

Look for examples of present perfect tense in magazines and newspapers and contrast them with text written in simple past tense. The verb is formed with 'has' or 'have'.

Brilliant Activities for Grammar and Punctuation, Year 3
© Irene Yates and Brilliant Publications

Assessment checklist

Name	1	2	3
Can understand and use the following terminology:			
Preposition			
Conjunction			
Word family			
Prefix			
Clause			
Subordinate clause			
Direct speech			
Consonant, consonant letter			
Vowel, vowel letter			
Inverted commas (or 'speech marks')			
Understands and is able to:			
Extend sentences with more than one clause by using a range of conjunctions, including 'when', 'if', 'because', 'although'.			
Change the tense of verbs from the past tense to the present tense			
Use conjunctions, adverbs and propositions to express time and cause			
Choose nouns or pronouns appropriately for clarity and cohesion and to avoid repetition			
Indicate possession by using the possessive apostrophe with plural nouns			
Understand the difference between direct and indirect speech			
Punctuate direct speech			
Form nouns using a range of prefixes			
Use the correct indefinite article (a/an) depending on whether the next word begins with a vowel or consonant			
Identify word families based on form and meaning			

Answers

All about vowels (pg 6)

miscellaneous, cauliflower, education, facetious.

eight, orange, far away, elephant, umbrella, carrot, alien, football, December, America.

Consonants (pg 7)

1. soldier 2. baker 3. farmer 4. butcher
5. pilot 6. fisherman 7. postperson 8. artist
9. doctor 10. mechanic.

Articles (pg 8)

A man is next door. It's a dog's basket. A bird, an apple, a baby, a boy, an ostrich, an elephant.

Which articles (pg 9)

I was on a picnic trip to the park. In my lunch box there was an apple, a banana, a sandwich and a little pack of cheese. The cheese was so hard to open, I knocked the whole lunch box to the ground and everything spilled out. A goose came up from nowhere. It snatched up the sandwich in its beak and waddled off. A duck came to see what it could find. It found a bit of ham, but as it dangled from its beak a different goose grabbed it from the duck and made off with it.

More pronouns (pg 11)

1. him 2. she 3. you 4. me 5. they 6. she
7. her 8. him.

Two problem pronouns (pg 12)

1. I 2. I 3. I 4. me

Collections (pg 16)

fruit, furniture, insects, birds

Lots of collections (pg 17)

Birds: sparrow, wren, thrush, hawk
Liquids: coffee, lemonade, wine, petrol
Family: aunt, grandad, cousin, niece
Games: football, golf, basketball, rugby
Numbers: one, two, nine, forty
Clothes: dress, shirt, jacket, pants
Vegetables: parsnip, carrot, cabbage, turnip
Flowers: daffodil, daisy, rose, tulip
Insects: ant, bee, fly, wasp

Animals: cow, dog, horse, donkey

More collections (pg 18)

people, trees, countries, food, salad, jewellery.
a class of students/children/pupils, a team of players, a bunch of bananas/flowers, a swarm of bees, a string of pearls, a pack of dogs/wolves.

Guess the prepositions (pg 20)

1. Up, 2. in, 3. off/from, 4. over, 5. down, 6. out.

More prepositions (pg 21)

The girls walked through the fields. A fox jumped over the fence. There was a hedgehog under a bush. There was a bird's nest in a tree. They climbed up a steep hill and laid the picnic blanket on the ground.

Preposition opposites (pg 22)

over/under, above/below, after/before, near/far, off/on, outside/inside.

Conjunctions (1) (pg 23)

We had to wait because the baby cried.
The kitten won't come to you unless you call it.
Dad said it would be all right if she bought the apple.
I will be there although I'll be late.
I cannot lift the bag because it is too heavy.
We'll have to dig our way out if it just keeps snowing.
He hasn't phoned me since I told him to go home.
We felt cold so we put the heating on.
The train was late but we got there on time.
Jaz can't come because she is grounded.

Simple sentences (pg 25)

Babies cry.	babies	cry
Boys climb.	boys	climb
Girls giggle.	girls	giggle
Teachers teach.	teachers	teach
Children learn.	children	learn
Trees grow.	trees	grow
Fish swim.	fish	swim
Ducks quack.	ducks	quack
Rain pours.	rain	pours
The Sun shines	the Sun	shines

Brilliant Activities for Grammar and Punctuation, Year 3
© Irene Yates and Brilliant Publications

Subjects and predicates (pg 26)

Dinosaurs — came to school on his bike.
You — are yellow.
A snake — must not be late for school.
The teacher — is long and slithery.
Bananas — gave us gold stars for our work.
My friend — are extinct.

Two clauses (pg 28)

I <u>had</u> ten books (and) I <u>read</u> them in the holidays.
I <u>like</u> oranges (but) I <u>love</u> bananas.
Their coats <u>got</u> wet (when) it <u>poured</u> with rain.
Our class <u>went</u> on a trip (and) we <u>had</u> a great time.

Complex sentences (pg 29)

<u>Jimmy ruined his shoes</u> when he paddled in them.
<u>We went to the circus</u> and saw the elephants dancing.
<u>The boy</u>, who broke his leg, <u>hobbled down the street</u>.
<u>We all got wet</u> when it rained.
When it snowed, <u>we built snowmen</u>.

Talking (pg 37)

"We're off to play football," he said.
"Can I come too?" she asked.
"Are you any good in goal?" he replied.
"Brilliant!" she said, "I saved six in our last game."
"Wow!" he said. "Join the team!"
"Now I'll show them!" she said.
<u>Note</u>: Pupils can attribute the speech to whoever they wish and use other verbs.

Direct or indirect? (pg 39)

	Direct	Indirect
"But I don't want to," Jack grumbled.	✓	
Mum said that was tough but he still had to go.		✓
Millie said he needed to get a grip.		✓
"I'll be too tired to play football with my mates," Jack moaned.	✓	
"Anyway, shopping's boring."	✓	
"It's boring for me as well," Mum snapped.	✓	
"And if there's nothing to seat you'll be moaning even more," Millie said.	✓	
Jack said he'd go but they'd have to wait while he got ready and texted his friend that he'd be late.		✓
"Just get a move on, will you?" Mum said.	✓	

Which is it? (pg 40)

1. Sahid said it was too hot for him today.
2. Maura said she hates chocolate.
3. "Who is you're friend?" asked Mum.
4. "I'm grounded," Ayesha said.
5. Sophie enquired what it was for.
6. "Sam isn't very well today," his dad said to Tom.
7. Millie said her favourite food is brocolli.
8. James thought the food was yucky.
9. "Why are you surprised?" the boy asked her.
10. Sam's dad told Tom he would take him to the match anyway.

Prefixes (pg 41)

<u>tri</u>o: a group of three; <u>tri</u>angle: a three sided object; <u>tri</u>ple: three times or three of; <u>tri</u>pod: on three legs; <u>tri</u>cycle: three wheeled bicycle; <u>tri</u>plet: set of three things;
<u>cent</u>: 100;
<u>oct</u>: eight,
<u>mille</u>: one thousand;
<u>duo</u>: two

Opposites (pg 42)

disappear, anticlimax, incapable.
Lots of words can be formed eg, unclear, disloyal, antistatic, inactive.
<u>un</u>: unseen, untie, unreal, unwilling, undo, unpaid, unroll, unsteady, unwise, unsafe.
<u>dis</u>: disagree, dislike, distrust, dishonest.

More prefixes (pg 43)

<u>super</u>: above, over, beyond
<u>auto</u>: self, one's own, automatic
<u>anti</u>: opposed to, against

Word families (pg 44)

run, ran, running, etc
nest, hive, burrow and any other animal home
said, called, yelled, spoke and others
synonyms *bicycle, skateboard*, scooter or any form of (non-motorised) transport

jump, jumping, jumped, etc

jump, hop, skip and similar words

write, written, wrote, etc.

rose, daffodil, tulip and any other flower.

Verb families (pg 45)

7 family groups:

run, runs, running, ran;

jog, jogs, jogging, jogged;

trot, trots, trotting, trotted;

bounce, bounces, bouncing, bounced;

swim, swims, swimming, swam;

climb, climbs, climbing, climbed;

skate, skates, skating, skated.

Lightning Source UK Ltd.
Milton Keynes UK
UKOW07f1054200316

270485UK00004B/24/P